Audrey White

Sally Ann Nichols

Buzzy Jellison

Buzzy Jellison

BUZZY JELLISON

The Funeral Home Cat

AUDREY M. WHITE

Illustrated by Sally Ann Nichols

First printed edition 2005
© AUDREY M. WHITE 2005
© Buzzy Jellison, © Buzzy, © Buzzy Jellison the Funeral Home Cat

ISBN 0-615-13000-3

Design & typesetting by Mullein Graphics
Illustrations © SALLY ANN NICHOLS 2005

To Meredith who, from the very beginning, felt that Buzzy's story needed to be told.

So many people have been enthusiastic in their support and help with the Buzzy project, as it became known:

Mr. Jellison who loves me, loves Buzzy but won't admit it, and cares deeply about the families he serves.

Sally Nichols who devoted so much of herself, her talent, and her time to Buzzy.

Mark Corsey, Ruth Linstromberg, Irv Richardson, and my children (all readers of the very first manuscript); Polly Bannister, Carol Betsch, and Coni Porter all of whom suggested and encouraged along with friends and family.

Maureen Rubino, whose heart broke when Buzzy left the restaurant business for the funeral home.

And of course Buzzy, who reminds us that all creatures can and do connect with one another—in the usual and some unusual ways.

My name is Buzzy Jellison, and I am a funeral home cat. I live above a funeral home with the owners, Mr. and Mrs. Jellison.

They had never had a cat until I arrived, so they were a little nervous about having a cat in a funeral home. Actually I was a little nervous about being a cat in a funeral home. Funeral homes are special places that take care of families and friends of people who die.

The funeral home itself is on the first floor of a big white house with black shutters. We live upstairs on the second and third floors. It's a home just like other people's homes.

I sleep in the living room on a special bed made just for me.

In the kitchen there is a cupboard where Mrs. Jellison keeps my favorite chicken-and-cheese-flavored treats; if I sit in front of the cupboard and look kind of hungry, she gives me one.

Downstairs, in the sunny front room, is where
Mr. Jellison meets with families to decide how
they will honor and celebrate the life of their
family member who has died. I like these
meetings because I learn interesting things
about the family. I sit at the top of the stairs
and listen a bit before coming downstairs to
introduce myself.

I can usually tell after a few minutes
on the stairs if the family would like
to be visited by a cat. If I don't think
they would, I just go back to sleep
upstairs in the living room, or I
have a little snack in the kitchen.
But mostly people are
happy to see me.

Sometimes I go with the visitors to the room where the urns are displayed or to the room where the caskets are displayed. These are pretty rooms where the families can see urns for ashes after a body has been cremated, or caskets for a body to be buried in.

Often they wander around and look at the colors and shapes and sizes. Often they know exactly which one would be perfect for the person who has died.

I like the swimming-dolphin urn and the black and gold casket. Sometimes they say, "What do you think, Buzzy Jellison?" and I let them know by walking over to the one I think would be right. Most of the time, it's the same one they like.

Some people have something of their own, like a teapot, in which they can put the ashes, and sometimes they want to make their own caskets. Mr. Jellison always says people should do whatever they think is right for the family.

Calling hours, sometimes called a "wake," is when the funeral home is set up with the urn or casket on display, and the family meets friends and relatives who will also miss the person who has died.

Sometimes I have been asked to come to calling hours. Mr. and Mrs. Jellison are a little curious about this, but I think I bring back good memories for families.

Many have had a cat that looked just like I do. Sometimes they just want someone's ears to scratch if their sadness has made it difficult to talk.

When calling hours start, I give the family a little time to be alone. I sit at the top of the stairs, listening.

While I'm waiting, I clean myself to make sure I look nice when I go downstairs.

I always go over to the family first
to let them know I'm there. Then I find a comfortable spot to watch
the people and to let them give my ears a little scratch when they go by.

I did have to get on top of a casket once because I knew that the man who had died loved cats a lot—I could smell his cats on his wool jacket. I didn't get into the casket, just sat on the top.

His family laughed and said that he would have loved that. Mr. Jellison was a little shocked when I did that, but he has calmed down now.

Another family asked if their dog could come to calling hours. I stayed upstairs that night.

The dog was very sad without his owner, and he needed to be alone with the family.

Many families make funeral plans before a family member dies. One such man was Mr. James. His mother knew she was dying, and she told him it was time for him to talk with Mr. Jellison. She told her son exactly how she wanted her calling hours and funeral to be conducted.

Mr. James is a very big man. He spoke in a very big voice, like this: "HELLO, MR. JELLISON. RALPH JAMES HERE. I AM HERE TO MAKE FUNERAL PLANS FOR MY MOTHER." He saw me and came over and lifted me up over his head and scratched my ears, and I really liked him. "SO YOU'RE BUZZY JELLISON? I'VE HEARD ABOUT YOU."

His mother died about a week later, and when he called he said, "MR. JELLISON? HOW'S THE CAT? I WOULD LIKE BUZZY TO COME TO MY MOTHER'S CALLING HOURS— IS THAT ALRIGHT WITH YOU, MR. JELLISON?" Of course it was, and I did go to the calling hours and I met the rest of his family, and they were all very big people with very big voices and THEY ALL LIKED ME!

Sometimes when people are placed into
their caskets, they are all dressed up in their
best clothes, but that's not always true.
Families bring in favorite clothes, which
are not always best clothes.

Many people tell their family members what
they want to wear. A grandfather wore his
Disney World shirt that his grandchildren
had given him. It had one of the Seven
Dwarves on it. Another man wore his jeans
and cowboy boots. A mother wore the dress
she had worn on her son's wedding day.
Lots of people are buried in their uniforms:
soldiers, policemen, and firemen.

And families put lots of different things into the caskets. A little girl was buried with her ice-skates. A man who played poker every week for many years had a deck of cards. A grandmother had a huge stuffed giraffe with her—her grandchildren had given it to her because they said all she ever talked about was her trip to Africa and how much she loved seeing the giraffes. And people put in photographs, awards, and other items (like candy bars!) that are special to them and the person they loved.

The saddest times are when children die. If a child dies of a sickness, his or her family has had a chance to say good-bye, and that helps the family a little bit.

If a child dies in an accident, I think it is more difficult for everyone, especially if the accident had to do with something dangerous that parents have warned their children about. Those parents and brothers and sisters and grandparents are so very sad.

Sometimes they are angry too that such an awful thing has happened to a child. All their hopes and dreams for that child are gone.

Mr. Jellison calls them often in the weeks and months after their child's death to see how they are. And he sends all his families a note on the one-year anniversary of their family member's death because he knows that date can be the saddest of all.

We serve families of many religions as well as those who do not have a religion. The traditions of the many religions are very interesting. Mr. Jellison knows a lot about each one. But when he does have a question, he has people he can call. Mrs. Boxer helps him with Jewish customs. Mrs. Olsen helps him with Mormon customs.

We served a family once that had arrived in this country from Cambodia. They had escaped during a war in their country. Their grandmother died, and they taught us much about their beliefs. They dressed their grandmother in a silk garment of green and white.

She looked beautiful.

We encourage people to bring personal items to display in the funeral home during calling hours. One family took down all our pictures from the walls and put up paintings done by their family member. Another family brought in all the uniforms their dad had worn in his career as a Green Beret soldier.

One family whose dad was a milkman had saved all the different kinds of milk bottles he had delivered in his many years delivering milk in our town. I sniffed around for a long time to see if any of them still had a tiny bit of cream on top, but none did.

The special car Mr. Jellison owns to carry a casket is called a hearse. His happens to be black, but they also can be silver, gray, white or dark blue. The hearse carries the casket to the cemetery or the church.

Just recently, though, the casket containing the body of a retired fire chief was taken to the church on the back of a big red antique fire truck.

We help people during a sad time. They always thank me when they leave. Mr. and Mrs. Jellison thank me too or say, "Good job, Buzzy" when a family tells us that we took good care of them. They seem more peaceful when they leave, and that makes us feel good.

Sometimes I see the families we have served when they are walking by the funeral home. They stop and scratch my ears—they always remember me. And I always remember them.